COMPREHENSION for Young Readers

Insect and Animal Factual Comprehension Stories

Written by Bev Heaton

Published by World Teachers Press®

Published with the permission of R.I.C. Publications Pty. Ltd.

First published by R.I.C. Publications Pty. Ltd., Perth, Western Australia.

Printed in the United States of America.

Order Number 2-5093
ISBN 1-58324-015-2

D E F G H 09 08 07 06 05

395 Main Street
Rowley, MA 01969
www.didax.com

COMPREHENSION for Young Readers

Insect and Animal Factual Comprehension Stories

Foreword

The focus of this book is to help reinforce the student's knowledge and understanding of the insect and animal world.

The book contains thirteen high-interest topics covering the literal, inferential and evaluative areas of questioning. The straightforward text and consistent layout make it easy for the student to concentrate on the task at hand. New vocabulary has been introduced in context thus making the text meaningful and at the same time extending the student's vocabulary. This is commonly known as the content areas.

Answers have been included to save you valuable time.

Contents

Teachers Notes

The following is a suggested lesson development using one section in this book. It is an example of how the activity could be introduced, developed and extended.

Introduction:

Brainstorm the students' prior knowledge of frogs. Record all responses on the chalkboard, even if they are incorrect. All responses can then be discussed and verified. Further research can be encouraged as a class to prove or disprove any responses.

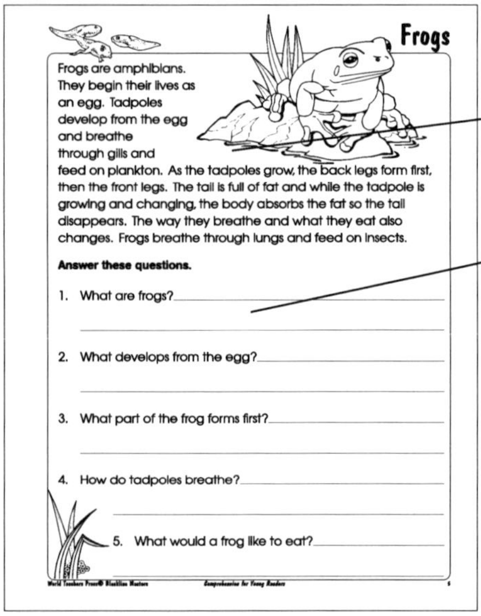

Frogs

Frogs are amphibians. They begin their lives as an egg. Tadpoles develop from the egg and breathe through gills and feed on plankton. As the tadpoles grow, the back legs form first, then the front legs. The tail is full of fat and while the tadpole is growing and changing, the body absorbs the fat so the tail disappears. The way they breathe and what they eat also changes. Frogs breathe through lungs and feed on insects.

Answer these questions.

1. What are frogs?
2. What develops from the egg?
3. What part of the frog forms first?
4. How do tadpoles breathe?
5. What would a frog like to eat?

Development:

1. Read through the passage with the whole group. Discuss any difficult language. Underline any key words as a group.

2. Discuss the questions and the type of answers required. Students can then write the answers on the page.

3. Discuss the fact that some questions only require a yes or no answer. Complete the yes/no responses and discuss students' answers. The students could then write some yes/no questions relating to frogs of their own.

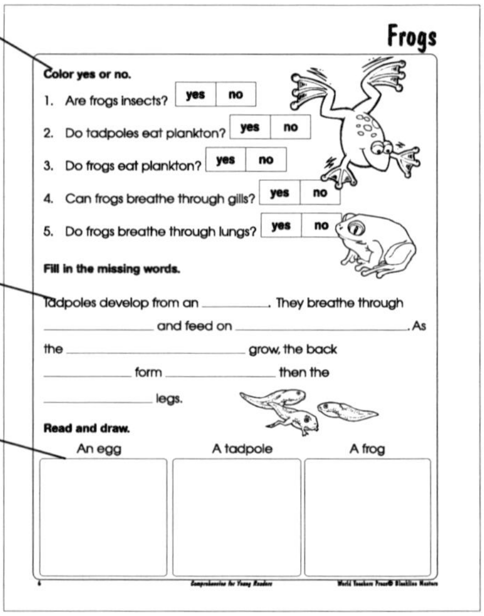

Frogs

Color yes or no.

1. Are frogs insects? yes no
2. Do tadpoles eat plankton? yes no
3. Do frogs eat plankton? yes no
4. Can frogs breathe through gills? yes no
5. Do frogs breathe through lungs? yes no

Fill in the missing words.

Tadpoles develop from an ________. They breathe through ________ and feed on ________. As the ________ grow, the back ________ form ________ then the ________ legs.

Read and draw.

An egg | A tadpole | A frog

4. Read through the cloze with the class and brainstorm possible words which could be used to complete the passage. This could also lead to a discussion on synonyms.

5. The final activity can be completed independently by the students.

Extension:

This lesson can be extended by students researching to find more frog facts, either independently or in small groups. A class book could be made to display all frog facts.

Frogs

Frogs are amphibians. They begin their lives as an egg. Tadpoles develop from the egg and breathe through gills and feed on plankton. As the tadpoles grow, the back legs form first, then the front legs. The tail is full of fat and while the tadpole is growing and changing, the body absorbs the fat so the tail disappears. The way they breathe and what they eat also changes. Frogs breathe through lungs and feed on insects.

Answer these questions.

1. What are frogs? ______________________________

____

2. What develops from the egg? ______________________________

____

3. What part of the frog forms first? ______________________________

____

4. How do tadpoles breathe? ______________________________

____

5. What would a frog like to eat? ______________________________

____

Color yes or no.

1. Are frogs insects? | yes | no |
2. Do tadpoles eat plankton? | yes | no |
3. Do frogs eat plankton? | yes | no |
4. Can frogs breathe through gills? | yes | no |
5. Do frogs breathe through lungs? | yes | no |

Fill in the missing words.

Tadpoles develop from an ____________. They breathe through ____________________ and feed on ________________________________. As the _________________________________ grow, the back ________________ form ____________________ then the ____________________ legs.

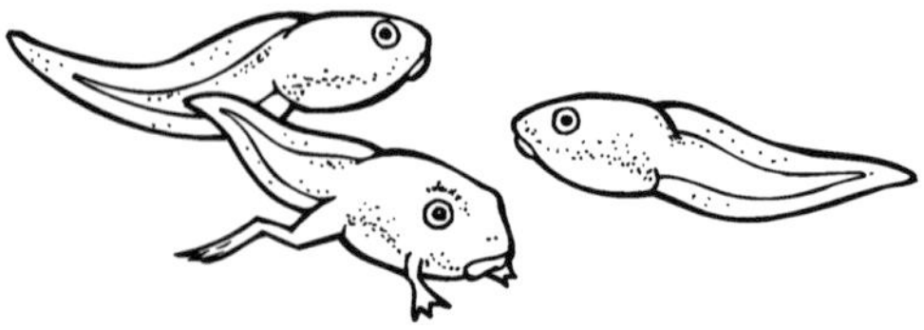

Read and draw.

An egg	A tadpole	A frog

Grasshoppers

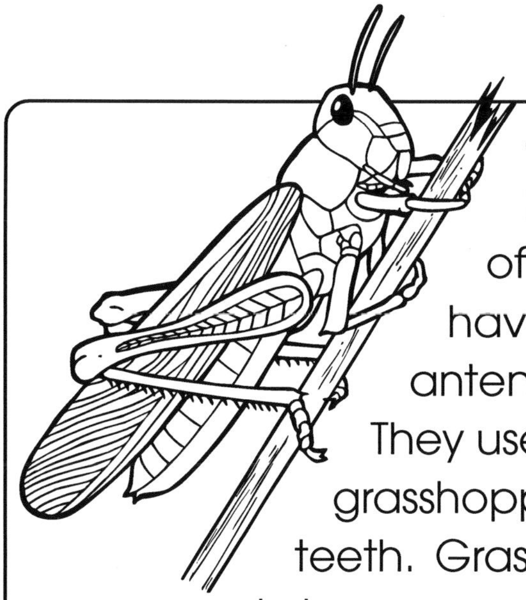

Grasshoppers are insects. They have six legs. Most grasshoppers have two pairs of wings but some grasshoppers don't have wings at all. Grasshoppers have two antennae joined at each side of their head. They use these to examine food. The grasshopper has two powerful jaws with sharp teeth. Grasshoppers can destroy whole crops when in large groups. They feed on plants and leaves.

Answer these questions.

1. What are grasshoppers? ______________________

____

2. How many legs do they have? ______________________

____

3. What do they use their antennae for? ______________________

____

4. What do grasshoppers eat? ______________________

____

5. When are grasshoppers pests?

____

____

Grasshoppers

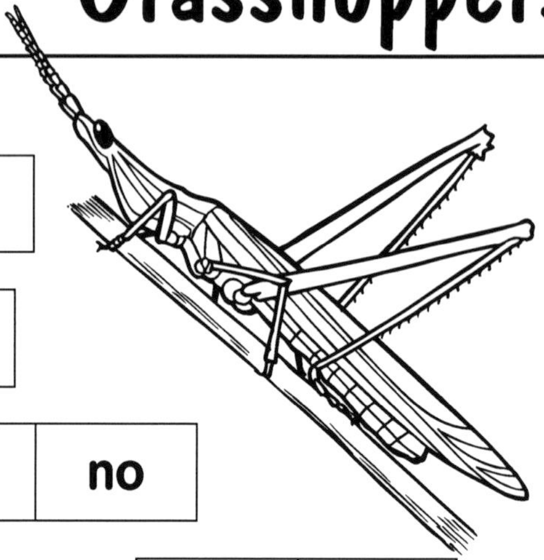

Color yes or no.

1. Are grasshoppers insects? | yes | no |
2. Do they have eight legs? | yes | no |
3. Do all grasshoppers have wings? | yes | no |
4. Can grasshoppers eat with their antennae? | yes | no |
5. Can grasshoppers destroy whole crops? | yes | no |

Fill in the missing words.

Grasshoppers are ____________________. They have ________ legs. Most grasshoppers have ________ pairs of ______________ but some ________________________ don't have ______________ at all.

Read and draw.

A grasshopper with two pairs of wings sitting on a green leaf.

Butterflies

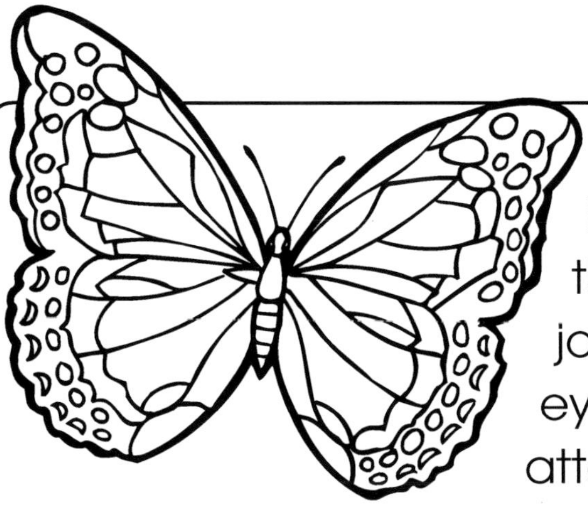

Butterflies are insects. Butterflies begin life as an egg. They have three parts to their body. The head has two antennae joined at each side and compound eyes. The butterfly has two pairs of wings attached to the thorax. The abdomen helps to store food. Butterflies drink nectar through a long tube called a proboscis.

Answer these questions.

1. What are butterflies? ____________________

   ____

2. How does a butterfly begin life? ____________________

   ____

3. How many body parts does a butterfly have? ____________________

   ____

4. What does the abdomen help to store? ____________________

   ____

   ____

5. How does a butterfly drink?

   ____

   ____

Butterflies

Color yes or no.

1.	Butterflies are insects.	yes	no
2.	Butterflies have three parts to their body.	yes	no
3.	Butterflies have two pairs of wings.	yes	no
4.	They store food in their abdomen.	yes	no
5.	The long tube used for drinking is a proboscis.	yes	no

Fill in the missing words.

Butterflies are ____________________. Butterflies begin ____________ as an _________. They have ______________ parts to their ____________. The head has __________ _________________________ joined at each side and _________________________ ____________.

Read and draw.

A butterfly sitting on a yellow flower drinking nectar.

Snails

Snails are mollusks. Their soft body is covered by a coiled shell. They have a head, two feelers, two eyes, a mouth and a tongue covered with tiny teeth.

Snails have one foot. The snail's foot moves it along in a backward, wavelike movement. Snails breathe through a hole in the side of their body. Snails live almost everywhere.

Answer these questions.

1. What are snails? ______________________________

____

2. What is their body covered with? ______________________________

____

3. How many feet does a snail have? ______________________________

____

4. How does a snail move? ______________________________

____

5. Where could you find a snail?

____

____

Color yes or no.

1. Are snails insects?	yes	no
2. Is their body covered by a shell?	yes	no
3. Do snails have one foot?	yes	no
4. Do snails breathe through a nose?	yes	no
5. Do snails live almost everywhere?	yes	no

Fill in the missing words.

Snails are ____________________. Their soft body is covered by a ________________ ________________. They have a __________, two __________________, two eyes, a _____________ and a tongue covered with tiny _____________.

Read and draw.

A snail sitting on a large flower.

Bees

Bees are hairy insects with wings. Bees feed on the nectar of flowers. They gather pollen from the flowers when it sticks on their legs and body. The proboscis, which is attached to the head, is used to drink the nectar. The worker bees change the nectar into honey. Bees live in colonies and there is only one queen. Bees live for only a few weeks.

Answer these questions.

1. What are bees? ______________________________

____

2. What do bees feed on? ______________________________

____

3. How do bees drink nectar? ______________________________

____

4. How long do bees live? ______________________________

____

5. Would you like to be a worker bee? ____________

Why/Why not? ______________________________

____

Bees

Color yes or no.

1. Are bees insects? | yes | no |
2. Is pollen gathered from flowers? | yes | no |
3. Is the proboscis attached to the head? | yes | no |
4. Does the queen bee change the nectar into honey? | yes | no |
5. Do bees live in colonies? | yes | no |

Fill in the missing words.

Bees are hairy ____________________ with ______________.

Bees feed on the ____________________ of

____________________. They gather ____________________

from the ____________________ when it sticks on their

____________ and ____________.

Read and draw.
A bee gathering
nectar from a flower.

Caterpillars

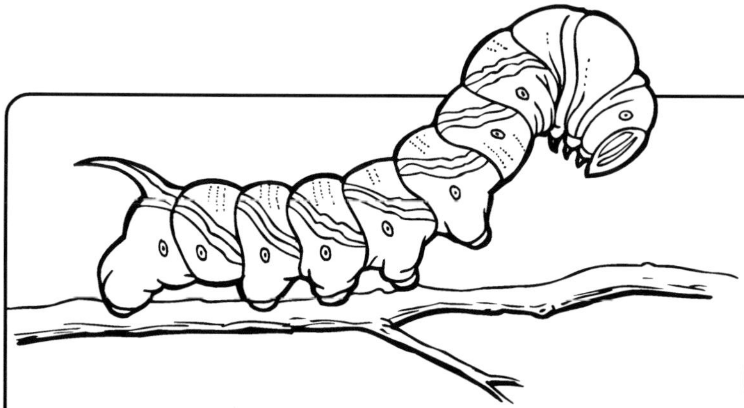

Caterpillars are wormlike creatures. They begin life as an egg. As the caterpillar grows it becomes too big for its skin. The skin splits and the caterpillar wriggles out. The caterpillar will change its skin about three more times. The caterpillar turns head down and clasps onto a tree or bush stem. It spins a silken girdle to attach it to the stem. The caterpillar is completely enclosed in its cocoon. It stays in that form until it develops into a butterfly or a moth.

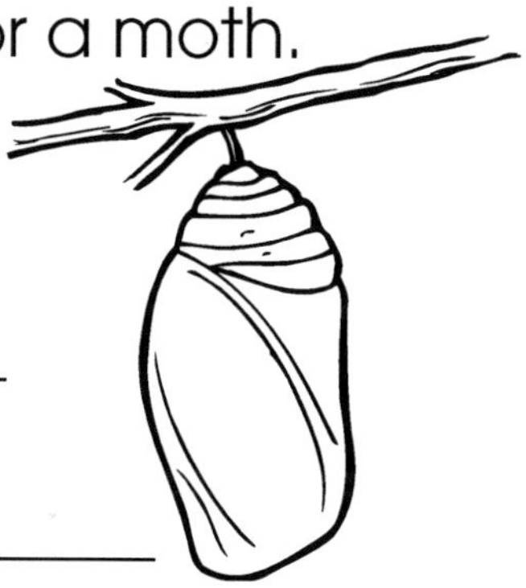

Answer these questions.

1. What are caterpillars?____________________________

____

2. How do caterpillars begin their life?____________________

____

3. What happens to its skin?________________________________

____

4. What does it spin?__________________________________

____

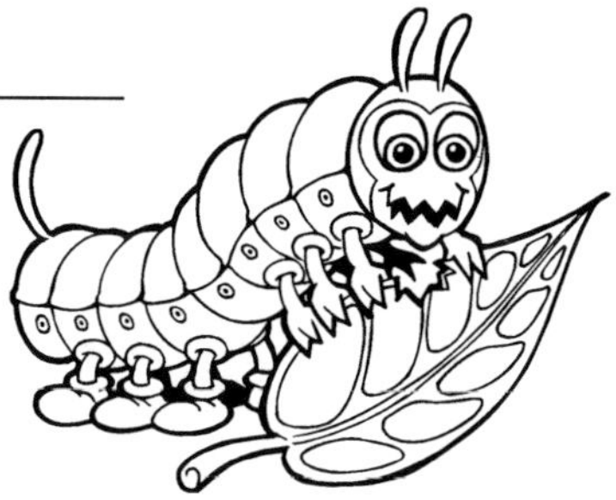

5. Do you like caterpillars? ____________________

Why/Why not?____

Color yes or no.

1. Do caterpillars begin life as an egg?

yes	no

2. Does the caterpillar's skin split?

yes	no

3. Does the caterpillar turn head down and clasp onto a stem?

yes	no

4. Is the caterpillar completely enclosed in its cocoon?

yes	no

5. Does the caterpillar turn into a worm

yes	no

Fill in the missing words.

Caterpillars are ______________________________ ______________________________. They begin ______________ as an ___________. As the caterpillar grows it becomes too ___________ for its ______________. The skin ______________________ and the ______________________________ wriggles out.

Read and draw.
Draw a caterpillar breaking out of its skin.

Ants

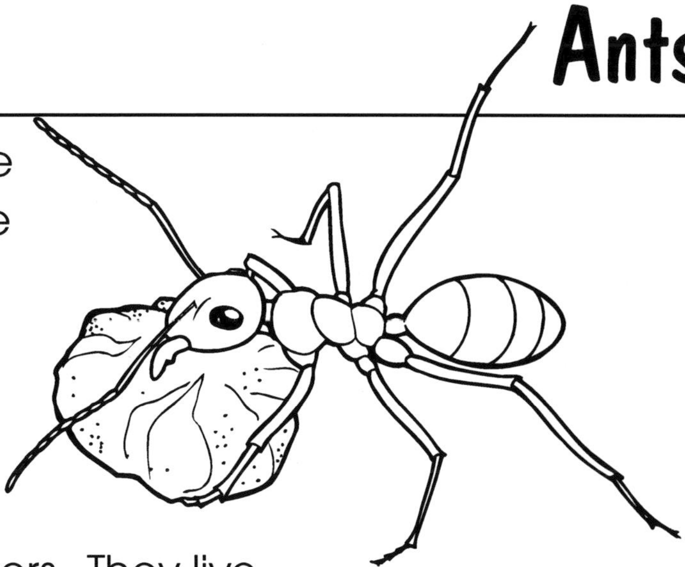

Ants are insects. There are three main parts to an ant. They have a head which has two antennae, a thorax which controls the movements of its six legs and an abdomen which stores its food. Ants dig nests which have many chambers. They live in colonies. Ants are found in all parts of the world except near the North and South Poles.

Answer these questions.

1. What is an ant? ______________________________

   ____

2. How many legs does an ant have? ______________________________

   ____

3. Name the three parts of an ant's body. ______________________________

   ______________________________ ______________________________

4. What do ants dig? ______________________________

   ____

5. Why do you think ants aren't found near the

   North and South Poles? ______________________________

   ____

Ants

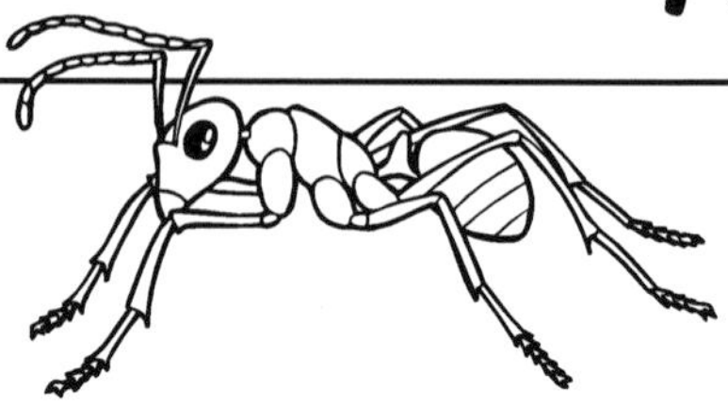

Color yes or no.

1. Are ants insects?	yes	no
2. Are there three main parts to an ant's body?	yes	no
3. Are the legs joined to the abdomen?	yes	no
4. Do ants dig nests?	yes	no
5. Do ants live near the North Pole?	yes	no

Fill in the missing words.

Ants are ______________________. There are three main ________________ to an __________ body. They have a _____________ which has two ____________________________, a ____________________ which controls the movement of its six _____________ and an _______________________ which stores food.

Read and draw.
Some ants digging a nest.

Mice

A mouse is a small mammal with soft fur. It has a pointed nose, round black eyes, rounded ears and a thin tail. A mouse is a rodent. A rodent's front teeth grow throughout the animal's life. Some mice are kept as pets. House mice live wherever people live. They often build nests in homes, garages, or sheds and steal food. Mice can climb anywhere and can be heard running through the ceiling.

Answer these questions.

1. What is a mouse?______________________________

____

2. What shape eyes do mice have?__________________

____

3. Where do house mice live?______________________

____

4. Where do mice build their nests?________________

____

5. Would you like a mouse as a friend?______________

Why/Why not?__________________________________

Color yes or no.

1. Does a mouse have soft fur?	yes	no
2. Do a rodent's front teeth stop growing?	yes	no
3. Are some mice kept as pets?	yes	no
4. Can mice build nests in the ceiling?	yes	no
5. Can a mouse climb everywhere?	yes	no

Fill in the missing words.

A mouse is a small ____________________ with soft __________. It has a pointed ______________, round ________________, rounded ______________ and a thin ______________.

Read and draw.

A mouse sitting in a nest in the garage.

Silkworms

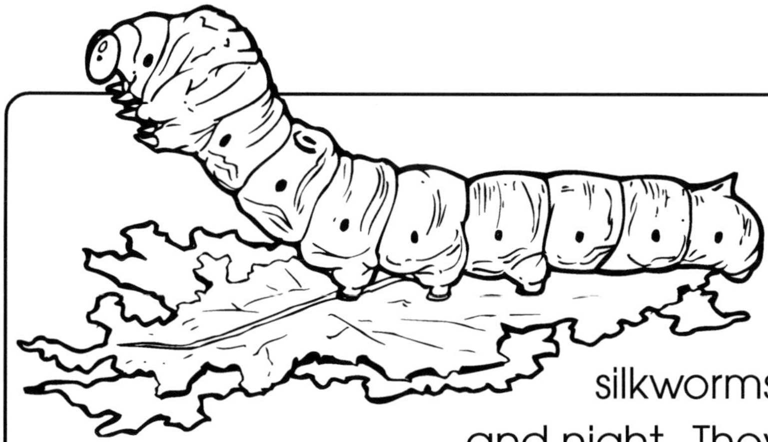

The female *Bombyx mori* moth lays between 300 and 500 eggs. The eggs hatch into tiny silkworms. The silkworms eat continually, both day and night. They feed on fresh mulberry leaves. When the silkworm has fully grown it has three pairs of legs. The silkworm stops eating. The worm spins a net to hold itself to a stem. It then spins its cocoon which is made of silk.

Answer these questions.

1. What is a *Bombyx mori* ?____________________

____

2. How many eggs does it lay?____________________

____

3. What do the eggs hatch into?____________________

____

4. What do silkworms feed on?____________________

____

5. How does the silkworm make silk?

____

____

Silkworms

Color yes or no.

1. Is a *Bombyx mori* a female moth? yes | no
2. Do the eggs hatch into tiny silkworms? yes | no
3. Do they feed on fresh gum leaves? yes | no
4. Does the silkworm have three pairs of legs? yes | no
5. Is the cocoon made of silk? yes | no

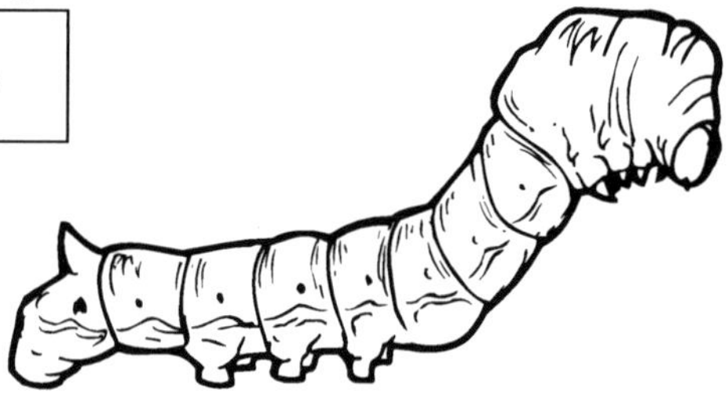

Fill in the missing words.

The female ______________ ______________ moth lays between 300 and 500 ______________. The eggs hatch into tiny ______________________. The silkworms eat continually, both __________ and ______________. They feed on fresh ______________________ leaves.

Read and draw.
A silkworm holding onto a leaf spinning its cocoon.

Mosquitoes

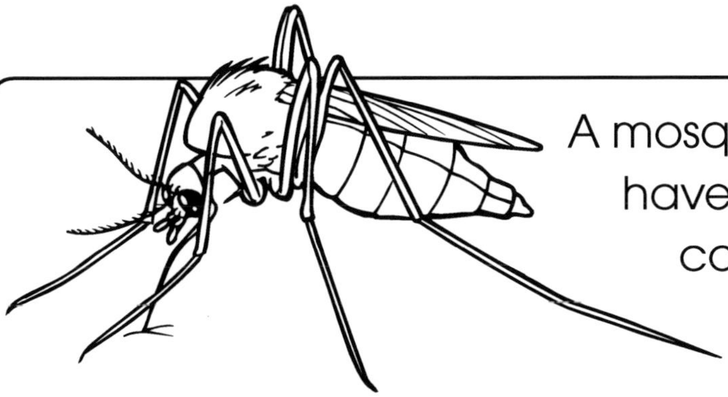

A mosquito is an insect. Mosquitoes have huge compound eyes which can see in different directions. The eyes are always open, even when it is asleep. A mosquito does not bite but stabs through the victim's skin and sucks the blood. The female needs the blood to feed the eggs inside her body. Once the eggs are laid, they turn into larvae. The larva turns into a pupa and finally it changes into a mosquito.

Answer these questions.

1. What are mosquitoes?______________________________

____

2. What type of eyes do mosquitoes have?________________

____

3. How does a mosquito reach the blood?________________

____

4. Why does the female mosquito need blood?______________________________

____

5. Why do you think mosquitoes sleep with their eyes open?

____

Mosquitoes

Color yes or no.

1. Do mosquitoes have compound eyes? | yes | no |
2. Can mosquitoes see in different directions? | yes | no |
3. Does a mosquito bite? | yes | no |
4. Does the male mosquito suck blood? | yes | no |
5. Do the eggs turn into larvae? | yes | no |

Fill in the missing words.

Mosquitoes have huge ______________________ eyes which can ________ in different ______________________. The ___________ are always ___________, even when it is ________________. A mosquito does not ___________, but ______________ the victim's skin and ______________ the blood.

Read and draw.
A mosquito sitting on your arm drinking your blood.

Chickens

A chicken is a bird. Chickens are the only birds that have combs. The comb is the red piece of flesh on top of the chicken's head. Chicken eggs take twenty-one days to hatch. Hens hatch their eggs by sitting on them to keep them warm. Hatcheries use hatching machines called incubators. Chickens are raised for meat, eggs and feathers.

Answer these questions

1. What is a chicken? ______________________________

____

2. What is a comb? ______________________________

____

3. How do hens hatch their eggs? ______________________________

____

4. What do hatcheries use to hatch eggs? ______________________________

____

5. Would you like to have a chicken for a pet?

______________ Why/Why not? ______________

____

Chickens

Color yes or no.

1. Is a chicken an insect? | yes | no |
2. Does it take ten days for the eggs to hatch? | yes | no |
3. Is a hatching machine called an incubator? | yes | no |
4. Does a chicken have a comb? | yes | no |
5. Are chickens raised for meat, eggs and feathers? | yes | no |

Fill in the missing words.

A chicken is a ______________. Chickens are the only ________________ that have ________________. The comb is the __________ piece of ________________ on __________ of the chicken's ______________.

Read and draw.

A hen sitting on six eggs in her nest.

Beetles

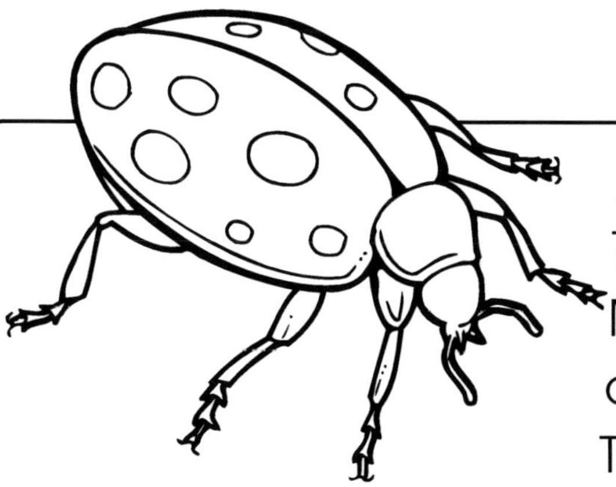

Beetles are insects. They have six legs. The ladybug is the best known beetle. Most beetles' bodies have tough walls of horny material on the underside. Thick wings cover the body. The hard body and the wings protect the beetle from birds or other enemies. The colors of most beetles are very bright. Some have patterns of stripes, dots, or splotches. The beetle begins life as an egg. It changes into a larva, then a pupa, and finally becomes the adult beetle.

Answer these questions.

1. What are beetles? ______________________________

____

2. Which is the best known beetle? ______________________________

____

3. What are most beetles' bodies made from? ______________________________

____

4. What covers the body? ______________________________

____

5. Do you like beetles? ____________________

Why/Why not? ______________________________

Beetles

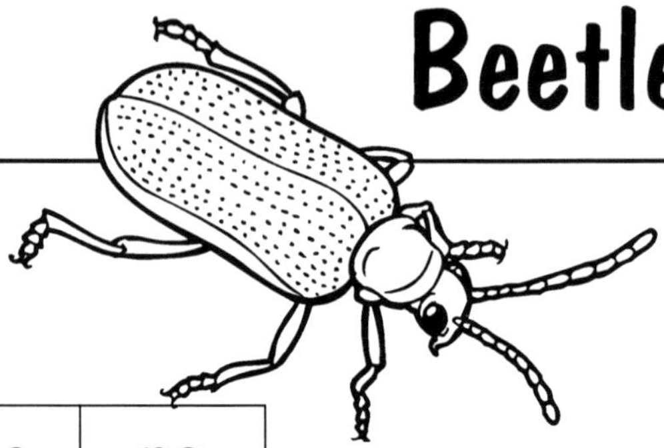

Color yes or no.

1.	Is a beetle an insect?	**yes**	**no**
2.	Does a beetle have eight legs?	**yes**	**no**
3.	Does the beetle's wings cover its body?	**yes**	**no**
4.	Do all beetles have dots?	**yes**	**no**
5.	Do most beetles have bright colors?	**yes**	**no**

Fill in the missing words.

Beetles are ______________________. They have ______________

______________. The ______________________ is the best

known ______________________. Most beetles' bodies have

______________ ______________ of ______________

material on the ______________________.

Read and draw.

A ladybug sitting on the stem of a flower.

Spiders

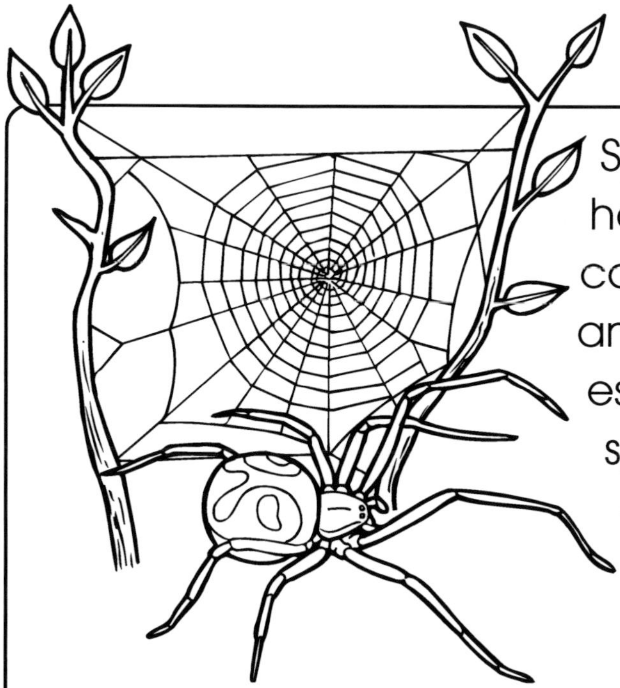

Spiders are not insects because they have eight legs. They spin silk webs to catch insects for food. Insects larger and stronger than the spider cannot escape from the spider's web. All spiders have fangs. A spider's bite can kill insects. Only a few spiders are harmful to humans. Spiders live anywhere they can find food.

Answer these questions.

1. Why aren't spiders insects? ____________________________

    ____

2. What kind of webs do spiders spin?

    ____

3. What do all spiders have? ____________

    ____

4. What do spiders eat? ____________________________

    ____

5. Why do you think insects cannot escape from the web?

    ____

    ____

Spiders

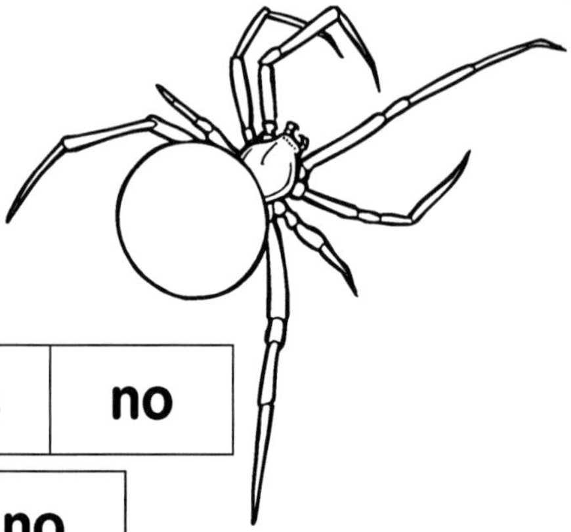

Color yes or no.

1. Are spiders insects? **yes** | **no**
2. Do spiders have six legs? **yes** | **no**
3. Do spiders catch food in their web? **yes** | **no**
4. Is the spider's web made of silk? **yes** | **no**
5. Are all spiders harmful to man? **yes** | **no**

Fill in the missing words.

Spiders are not ____________________ because they have ______________ ______________. Spiders spin silk ______________ to catch ____________________ for food. Insects larger and ______________________ than the ____________________ cannot ____________________ from the spider's ______________.

Read and draw.

A spider sitting in his web. A fly on the edge of the web.

Answers

Page 5 – Frogs
1. Frogs are amphibians.
2. A tadpole develops from the egg.
3. The back legs form first.
4. Tadpoles breathe through gills.
5. Answers will vary.

Page 6 – Frogs
1. No 2. Yes 3. No
4. No 5. Yes
Missing words: egg, gills, plankton, tadpoles, legs, first, front

Page 7 - Grasshoppers
1. Grasshoppers are insects.
2. They have six legs.
3. They use their antennae to examine food.
4. They eat plants and leaves.
5. They are pests when they destroy crops.

Page 8 – Grasshoppers
1. Yes 2. No 3. No
4. No 5. Yes
Missing words: insects, six, two, wings, grasshoppers, wings

Page 9 – Butterflies
1. Butterflies are insects.
2. It begins life as an egg.
3. It has three body parts.
4. It helps to store food.
5. It drinks through a long tube called a proboscis.

Page 10 – Butterflies
1. Yes 2. Yes 3. Yes
4. Yes 5. Yes
Missing words: insects, life, egg, three, body, two, antennae, compound eyes

Page 11 – Snails
1. Snails are mollusks.
2. It is covered by a coiled shell.
3. A snail has one foot.
4. It moves in a backward, wavelike way.
5. Answers will vary.

Page 12 – Snails
1. No 2. Yes 3. Yes
4. No 5. Yes
Missing words: mollusks, coiled shell, head, feelers, mouth, teeth

Page 13 – Bees
1. Bees are hairy insects with wings.
2. Bees feed on the nectar of flowers.
3. They drink nectar with a proboscis.
4. Bees live for only a few weeks.
5. Answers will vary.

Page 14 – Bees
1. Yes 2. Yes 3. Yes
4. No 5. Yes
Missing words: insects, wings, nectar, flowers, pollen, flowers, legs, body

Page 15 – Caterpillars
1. Caterpillars are wormlike creatures.
2. They begin life as an egg.
3. The skin splits when the caterpillar grows too big.
4. It spins a silken girdle or cocoon.
5. Answers will vary.

Page 16 – Caterpillars
1. Yes 2. Yes 3. Yes
4. Yes 5. No
Missing words: wormlike, creatures, life, egg, big, skin, splits, caterpillar

Page 17 – Ants
1. An ant is an insect.
2. An ant has six legs.
3. The head, the thorax and abdomen.
4. Ants dig nests which have many chambers.
5. Answers will vary.

Page 18 – Ants
1. Yes 2. Yes 3. No
4. Yes 5. No
Missing words: insects, parts, ant's, head, antennae, thorax, legs, abdomen

Page 19 – Mice
1. A mouse is a small mammal.
2. Mice have round eyes.
3. House mice live wherever people live.
4. They build nests in homes, garages, or sheds.
5. Answers will vary.

Page 20 – Mice
1. Yes 2. No 3. Yes
4. Yes 5. Yes
Missing words: mammal, fur, nose, black, eyes, ears, tail

Page 21 – Silkworms
1. A *Bombyx mori* is a moth.
2. It lays between 300 and 500 eggs.
3. The eggs hatch into silkworms.
4. They feed on mulberry leaves.
5. It spins a cocoon made of silk.

Page 22 – Silkworms
1. Yes 2. Yes 3. No
4. Yes 5. Yes
Missing words: *Bombyx mori*, eggs, silkworms, day, night, mulberry

Page 23 – Mosquitoes
1. Mosquitoes are insects.
2. They have compound eyes.
3. It stabs through the victim's skin.
4. It needs blood to feed the eggs.
5. Answers will vary.

Page 24 – Mosquitoes
1. Yes 2. Yes 3. No
4. No 5. Yes
Missing words: compound, see, directions, eyes, open, asleep, bite, stabs, sucks

Page 25 – Chickens
1. A chicken is a bird.
2. A comb is a red piece of flesh on the head.
3. They sit on the eggs to keep them warm.
4. They use incubators.
5. Answers will vary.

Page 26 – Chickens
1. No 2. No 3. Yes
4. Yes 5. Yes
Missing words: bird, birds, combs, red, flesh, top, head

Page 27 – Beetles
1. Beetles are insects.
2. The ladybug is the best known beetle.
3. A tough wall of horny material.
4. Thick wings cover the body.
5. Answers will vary.

Page 28 – Beetles
1. Yes 2. No 3. Yes
4. No 5. Yes
Missing words: insects, six, legs, ladybug, beetle, tough, walls, horny, underside

Page 29 – Spiders
1. Because they have eight legs.
2. Spiders spin silk webs.
3. All spiders have fangs.
4. Spiders eat insects.
5. Answers will vary.

Page 30 – Spiders
1. No 2. No 3. Yes
4. Yes 5. No
Missing words: insects, eight legs, webs, insects, stronger, spider, escape, web